GRANDPA

I WANT TO HEAR ABOUT

YOUR

LIFE

Grandpa, I Want to Hear About Your Life
© 2025 Casey Parker
All rights reserved.

Designed with love for grandfathers and their children.

Published by Midsummer Bloom Books

First Edition: March 2025
Printed in the United States of America

Contents

Your Stories Are Family Treasures

You know that look on your grandkids' faces when you start telling stories about the "good old days"? Yeah, that one - where their eyes get big and they scoot a little closer. Maybe it happens on a lazy Sunday when you're flipping through old photo albums, or just hanging out on the porch. Those stories of yours? They're like time machines for them, taking them back to a world that seems almost make-believe now.

Here's the thing - this book? It's more than just pages to write on. It's for keeping those stories alive, not just for your grandkids, but for their kids too someday. Because let's face it, you've got some pretty amazing memories stored up there: running around neighborhoods that don't even exist anymore, going to schools that were nothing like they are today, working those first jobs where you made pocket change by today's standards. The kind of stuff that makes your grandkids say "No way!"

Sure, they know you as Grandpa - the pancake master, the joke teller, the fix-it guy. But man, you've seen some changes. Remember when technology was so different in your day? Now these kids navigate their digital world like it's second nature! From the entertainment of your youth to today's streaming services - you've watched the world transform right before your eyes.

Just write it all down here - the trouble you got into as a kid, growing up, falling in love, all those jobs and life lessons.

Don't sweat the small stuff like spelling or if your writing's a bit messy. That's not what matters.

Take it easy - no rush. Just fill it up with the good stuff, the stuff that'll help them understand where they came from. Because someday, when they're older and reading this, they'll have something better than any gift you could buy - they'll have your story.

So, what do you say, Grandpa? Ready to share those adventures? Your grandkids are all ears!

How to Use This Book

Throughout this book, you'll find thought-starters and memory prompts beneath each question. These are simply suggestions to spark ideas and memories - feel free to use them as inspiration or take your story in completely different directions. There are no right or wrong ways to share your life stories here. Just enjoy looking back on the path that led you here.

Hey Grandpa, with your knowing smile,

Those hands that built a thousand things,

Your stories stretch back mile by mile,

Through time that's passed on gentle wings.

Come share your world - we're ready to listen.

1

When Times Were Simple

Deep roots stretch back through generations, each branch telling tales of triumph and tears. Who were these faces in faded photographs that shaped our family's story?

Family Roots

Our family tree stretches across generations. Some came from distant lands, others worked this soil for generations, all contributing to who we became.

Tell us about your family's heritage and background. What countries or regions did your ancestors come from, and what traditions did they bring with them?

What did your grandparents tell about their homeland?

• Home country

• Old traditions

When did our family first arrive here?

• Moving date

• Travel story

Which language memories stayed with family?

• Native words

• Speaking history

Father's Trade

My father's hands taught me that a man's worth isn't measured by his wealth, but by the pride he takes in his daily labor.

What kind of work did your father do? Describe his occupation, work ethic, and how his career shaped your family's daily life and your own understanding of responsibility.

What interesting stories did your father share about his work?

• Job tales

• Work life

What specific tasks and responsibilities did your father handle in his job?

• Daily work

• Main tasks

How did your father learn the skills needed for his profession?

• Skills learned

• Experience built

Mother's Ways

"A mother's love is the fuel that enables a normal human being to do the impossible." - Marion C. Garretty

How did your mother care for the family? Remember her daily routines, special touches, and the ways she made your childhood home feel special.

What particular routines did your mother follow to organize each day?

• Daily schedule

• Regular tasks

How did your mother handle household tasks and cooking duties?

• Cooking ways

• House care

Which skills or talents made your mother's care unique?

• Unique talents

• Special ways

The Family Home

"A house is made of walls and beams; a home is built with love and dreams." – Unknown

Paint a picture of your childhood home. What did it look like, feel like, and what special spots do you remember most clearly?

What made your childhood house special?

• House details

• Unique parts

Which room held most activities?

• Family space

• Main area

What surrounded your childhood home?

• House area

• Neighborhood view

Brothers & Sisters

Growing up with siblings meant sharing more than space - we shared secrets, adventures, quarrels, and reconciliations. They were my first friends and lifelong allies.

Who were your siblings and what was life like together? Share about your place in the family order and the adventures you shared.

What are your siblings' full names and stories behind them?

• Full names

• Name stories

What kind of games or activities did you enjoy together?

• Fun times

• Play together

How were household chores divided among siblings?

• Work split

• Task division

Extended Family

Aunts, uncles, cousins – each relative added their own flavor to our family story, their own thread to our tapestry.

Remember the special relatives who influenced your early years and family gatherings.

Which aunt or uncle influenced you most?

• Special aunt/uncle

• Life lessons

What made family gatherings memorable?

• Big events

• Together times

Which relative's house was special?

• Favorite house

• Visit memories

Childhood Meals

What foods filled your childhood table? Describe the meals, cooking traditions, and special dishes that bring back early memories.

What regular dishes appeared most often at family meals?

• Regular food

• Daily meals

How were special occasion meals different from everyday ones?

• Holiday food

• Party dishes

What mealtime rules and customs did your family follow?

• Table rules

• Eating ways

Holiday Memories

Holidays were times when family traditions shone brightest, when simple celebrations created lasting memories.

What made holidays special in your early years? Remember the celebrations that brought joy to your childhood.

Which holidays were most important in your family calendar?

• Big days

• Family events

Which holiday decorations and customs do you remember clearly?

• Decorations

• Traditions

How did gift-giving or special exchanges work in your family?

• Present giving

• Special exchanges

Neighborhood Life

Our neighborhood was its own small world - where everyone knew everyone, where doors stayed unlocked, where community meant something real and tangible.

What was your childhood community like? Describe the streets, neighbors, and daily life in the place where you grew up.

What were the main landmarks and gathering spots nearby?

• Key spots

• Meeting places

How did neighbors interact and help each other?

• Help ways

• Community ties

What local shops and services did families regularly use?

• Nearby shops

• Used services

Family Heroes

Every family has its heroes - some wore uniforms, others work clothes, but all showed courage in their own ways. These were the people who shaped our values.

Which family members did you especially admire? Tell us about the relatives who inspired you in your early years.

What stories about family heroes were often retold?

• Brave tales

• Family legends

What unique talents did your family heroes possess?

• Special skills

• Great abilities

Which life lessons did they teach you directly?

• Taught wisdom

• Life advice

Simple Treasures

Not every valuable thing shines like gold. Some treasures in your childhood home were passed down through generations, carrying worth in memories rather than money.

What family heirlooms meant the most to you as a child? Describe the special items or keepsakes in your childhood home that held deep meaning.

What handmade family items did you treasure growing up?

• Items crafted by relatives

• Traditional family pieces

Which family collections did you admire in your childhood home?

• Precious mementos

• Heritage items

How did you interact with these family treasures as a child?

• Special occasions

• Family stories shared

2

Early Days & Adventures

Skinned knees and summer breeze, the world was endless possibility. Through your childhood eyes, even the backyard became an unexplored wilderness waiting for its hero.

Boy's Daily Life

"The days of a child are long, but the years are short." – Unknown

What was a typical day like when you were very young? Remember your morning routines, daily activities, and the simple rhythm of childhood life.

What games did you play most often before starting school?

• Street games

• Backyard fun

What rules did you have to follow at home as a small boy?

• Sleep times

• Good behavior

Where did you like to go with your family on regular days?

• Shop trips

• Walk places

Outdoor Explorer

The outdoors was our playground - climbing trees, building forts, discovering nature's secrets. Every day brought new adventures in fields and hidden corners of the neighborhood.

Where did your outdoor adventures take you? Tell us about climbing trees, exploring yards, and discovering the world around your home.

What places near your home did you like to explore most?

• Hidden places

• Found spots

What outdoor activities filled your summer days?

• Water play

• Field fun

What animals or creatures did you often encounter outside?

• Pet friends

• Wild creatures

Treasured Toys

> *Our toys were simpler but built to last - wooden trucks, blocks, and trains that sparked imagination.*

What were your favorite playthings? Describe the toys that filled your early years, especially the simple ones that sparked imagination.

What was your most treasured toy before starting school?

• Special toy

• Favorite thing

How did you get most of your toys back then?

• Family gifts

• Handmade items

What toys did you wish for but never had?

• Dream toys

• Never had

Childhood Buddies

"A friend is one of the nicest things you can have and one of the best things you can be." – Douglas Pagels

Who were your first friends? Remember the playmates who shared your early adventures and the games you enjoyed together.

Who was your very first friend that you remember?

- First buddy

- Early friend

What games did you regularly play together?

- Play games

- Fun together

Where did you usually meet your childhood friends?

- Play spots

- Friend places

Sports & Games

Physical play wasn't organized then - it was spontaneous baseball games, street hockey, capture the flag. We made our own rules and solved our own disputes.

What active games filled your days? Describe the physical activities and energetic play that kept you moving.

What running or chasing games did you play most?

• Chase games

• Race types

What physical skills were you proud of mastering?

• Climb skills

• Balance acts

Where did you find good spaces for active play?

• Game spots

• Active areas

Building Things

Early projects taught more than construction - they built confidence, problem-solving skills, and the satisfaction of creating something with your own hands.

What did you enjoy creating or constructing? Share about early projects, from sandcastles to toy buildings, that showed your creativity.

What materials were easily available for building?

• Found stuff

• Nature items

What did you like making from wooden pieces?

• Block builds

• Stick makes

Where did you keep your finished projects?

• Show spots

• Keep places

Young Collector

Boys collect treasures others might overlook - interesting rocks, bottle caps, baseball cards. Each item held stories in a young boy's world.

What treasures did you gather as a boy? Describe the special items you collected and saved, from rocks to bottle caps to trading cards.

What natural items did you like collecting outdoors?

• Pretty rocks

• Special leaves

Which items did other kids like trading with you?

• Trade items

• Exchange things

What collection made you most proud back then?

• Proud pieces

• Special sets

Boy's Clothes

Clothes were made for adventure then - patches on knees, shoes scuffed from play, pockets full of treasures. We wore our activities in the wear and tear.

What did young boys wear in your day? Remember the typical outfits, special occasion clothes, and how different it was from today.

What did you usually wear for everyday play?

• Daily wear

• Regular clothes

How were your special occasion clothes different?

• Church best

• Party wear

What kind of shoes did young boys have then?

• Shoe kinds

• Foot wear

After Dark

What made evenings special? Tell us about nighttime routines, evening activities, and the magic of dusk in your childhood.

What was your regular bedtime routine like?

• Night steps

• Sleep prep

What activities did your family share after dinner?

• Night games

• Family fun

What stories or songs were part of bedtime?

• Sleep tales

• Night songs

3

Lessons & Schoolyard Tales

Chalk dust and paper planes, strict teachers and best friends. Between classroom walls and playground fences, you learned about more than just books and numbers.

First School Day

That first morning remains clear – new shoes squeaking on wooden floors, the smell of chalk dust, desks in neat rows.

What do you remember about your very first day of school? Share about your feelings, what you wore, and how different school life was from home.

What did you wear on your first day?

- Special clothes

- School bag

Who took you to school that first morning?

- Who took you

- Morning goodbye

What feelings do you remember from that day?

- Morning nerves

- New friends

Favorite Teachers

Which teachers left a lasting impression? Tell us about the teachers who inspired you and the lessons that stuck with you.

Who was your favorite teacher, and what made your best teacher different from the others?

• Special teacher

• Great teaching

What interesting things did this teacher show your class?

• Cool learning

• Fun projects

How did this teacher make difficult subjects easier?

• Easy ways

• Clear steps

Best Friends

"A friend is one who knows you and loves you just the same." - El-bert Hubbard

Who were your closest school friends? Remember the special buddies who shared your school years and the adventures you had together.

How did you meet your best school friend?

• First hello

• Friend start

What games or activities did you enjoy together?

• Playing together

• Shared fun

What mischief did you sometimes get into?

• Little pranks

• Silly times

Sports Teams

Team sports taught more than just games - they built character, showed the power of working together, taught us how to win gracefully and lose with dignity.

What sports did you play in school? Describe your experiences on teams, memorable games, and the camaraderie you shared with teammates.

What sports teams did you try out for in school?

• Sport choice

• Team tryouts

What positions did you play on your teams?

• Game spot

• Team role

What game or match do you remember most?

• Big game

• Great plays

After School Life

When classes ended, adventures began. These hours between school and dinner shaped our independence.

What filled your hours after the school bell? Remember your activities and how you balanced homework with play time.

What was your usual route home from school?

• Home path

• Walk friends

Where did you and friends hang out after school?

• Friend places

• Play areas

How did you balance homework and play time?

• Study time

• Play time

Class Projects

Some assignments became more than homework - science fair volca-noes, history presentations, art projects that pushed creativity beyond textbook learning.

What school assignments stand out in your memory? Describe special projects, presentations, or assignments that made learning memorable.

What was your most interesting science project?

• Lab work

• Cool finds

How did you make presentations without computers?

• Display methods

• Show tools

Which art or craft projects were most fun?

• Making art

• Craft fun

School Adventures

Field trips and special events broke routine - museum visits, class performances, outdoor education days that turned learning into excitement.

What exciting events happened at school? Share about field trips, special programs, or unexpected moments that broke the routine.

What was your most memorable school field trip?

- Trip place

- Group fun

What exciting school events happened each year?

- School shows

- Big days

Which school visitors made a big impression?

- Guest talks

- New people

Competition Days

"The most important thing is not winning but taking part." - *Pierre de Coubertin*

How did you experience school competitions? Tell about sports matches, academic contests, or other competitive events you participated in.

What school competitions did you take part in?

- Competition type

- Taking part

How did you prepare for big competitions?

- Practice ways

- Mind prep

What was your most exciting victory moment?

- Victory moment

- Happy time

Achievement Pride

Success came in many forms – academic awards, athletic victories, personal bests. Each achievement built confidence for the next challenge.

What accomplishments made you proud? Tell about awards or personal victories that boosted your confidence in school.

What was your first major school achievement?

• Early win

• Proud time

Which skill improvement made you most proud?

• Better skill

• Learning growth

What recognition did you receive from teachers?

• Good praise

• Class reward

4

Building Your Path

Standing at life's crossroads, you carved your own way forward. Young dreams met reality as independence taught its first hard-won lessons about becoming your own man.

First Journey Alone

Independence arrives like a train pulling from the station - slowly at first, then steadily carrying you to new horizons.

Remember that first solo trip - navigating unfamiliar places with just your wits and courage.

When did you first venture out into the world alone? Think about:

• Where you went

• Main places

What feelings accompanied those first independent steps? Remember:

• First fears

• Free feeling

How did traveling on your own reshape how you saw the world? Consider:

• Changed thoughts

• Fresh eyes

First Job Dreams

"The future belongs to those who believe in the beauty of their dreams." – Eleanor Roosevelt

What kind of work did you imagine doing when you were young? Share about your early career aspirations and how they shaped your path.

What kind of work did you first want to do when you were young?

• Dream occupation

• Salary hopes

How did you learn about different job choices back then?

• Career info

• Local jobs

Which jobs were most popular among young people then?

• Common jobs

• Hot careers

First Apartment

That first space of my own was modest but felt like a palace. It wasn't much, but it was mine, earned with my own work.

What was it like setting up your first place? Remember the excitement and challenges of living on your own for the first time.

Where did you find your first place to live alone?

• Home type

• Monthly cost

What furniture and items did you start with?

• Must-haves

• Start items

What were your biggest challenges living alone?

• Daily needs

• New learn

Bachelor Days

Independence meant learning life's basics. These simple freedoms taught responsibility alongside celebration of being my own man.

How did you enjoy your independence? Tell about the freedom, responsibilities, and adventures of your early adult years.

What was your typical daily schedule like?

• Work day

• Life flow

What did you usually do on weekends back then?

• Free days

• Friend time

Where did you go for entertainment?

• Fun spots

• Night out

Own Transport

"The car has become the carapace, the protective and aggressive shell, of urban and suburban man." - *Marshall McLuhan*

What was your first vehicle? Share the story of your first car or motorcycle - how you got it, maintained it, and the freedom it brought.

What was your first vehicle and how did you choose it?

• Vehicle type

• Purchase story

What repairs or problems did you handle?

• Common issues

• Fix attempts

Where did you travel with your vehicle?

• Drive places

• Road fun

Money Lessons

Managing my own money taught practical wisdom - the value of saving and the security of planning ahead. These lessons shaped life-long habits.

How did you learn to manage your finances? Remember the early lessons about budgeting, saving, and handling your own money.

What were the best money tips you learned?

- Smart save

- Good spend

How different were prices and costs then?

- Life costs

- Money then

What big purchases did you save for?

- Save goals

- Major needs

Life Skills

Independence required mastering many skills – from fixing leaky faucets to balancing checkbooks. Each new ability built confidence and self-reliance.

What essential skills did you develop? Tell about learning to cook, maintain a home, and handle adult responsibilities.

What basic home repairs did you learn to handle?

• Fix work

• Tool use

What were your laundry and cleaning routines?

• Wash ways

• House clean

How did you organize your paperwork and bills?

• Bill file

• Keep track

Early Work Days

First steps into working life taught more than job skills - they showed the value of punctuality, reliability, and the satisfaction of earning your way.

What was your first real job like? Share about your initial work experiences, the environment, and adjusting to professional life.

What was your first day at work like?

• Start job

• First work

What skills did you need to learn quickly?

• Must learn

• Fast grasp

How did you handle your first workplace challenges?

• Job fix

• Task solve

Success Stories

Early achievements built confidence - first promotion, customer praise, problems solved. Each success led to the next.

What early career achievements made you proud? Remember the accomplishments that built your confidence in the working world.

What was your first big success at work?

- Major achievement

- Recognition moment

How did you earn your first promotion?

- Work effort

- Position change

What work skills made you stand out?

- Special talents

- Unique abilities

Challenge Times

Obstacles weren't roadblocks but learning opportunities – each challenge overcome made the next one easier to face with determination and wisdom gained.

How did you handle early career obstacles? Tell about difficulties you faced and how you overcame them.

What was your biggest early work challenge?

- Hard task

- Fix need

How did you deal with difficult coworkers?

- People problems

- Conflict handling

What mistakes taught you important lessons?

- Mistakes

- Learning moments

Career Choices

"Choose a job you love, and you will never have to work a day in your life." - Confucius

What influenced your job decisions? Share about the turning points and choices that directed your career path.

What career changes did you make?

• New job

• Field change

What opportunities surprised you most?

• Good chance

• Surprise win

How did location affect your job choices?

• Move choice

• Job spot

Mentor Stories

Who helped guide your career path? Remember the people who offered wisdom, advice, and support in your professional journey.

Who taught you the most at your first job?

- Key teacher

- Work guidance

What was the best advice you received?

- Wise words

- Smart tips

How did mentors change your career?

- Growth aid

- Career path

Business Wisdom

Work taught lasting lessons - about integrity in small things, the value of reputation, the importance of relationships over transactions.

What key lessons did you learn about work? Remember the insights that proved most valuable in your professional life.

What important rules about work proved true?

• Success rules

• Work facts

What business habits served you best?

• Work routines

• Success habits

How did you spot good opportunities?

• Success signs

• Growth chances

5

When Life Changed Forever

Love struck like lightning - sudden, bright, and transforming. The moment you met Grandma, your solo journey became a duet that would last a lifetime.

First Crush

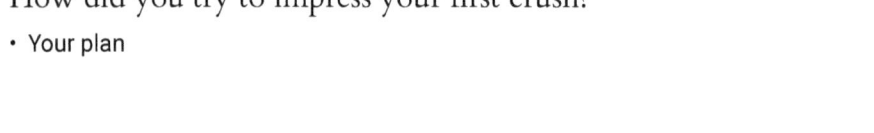

Young hearts learn their first lessons about love in unexpected ways. Remember that special someone who first made your heart skip a beat?

Tell us about those innocent feelings of young love and what memories have stayed with you all these years.

How did you try to impress your first crush?

• Your plan

• How it turned out

What's the most embarrassing situation you found yourself in with an early sweetheart?

• What happened

• Others' reactions

Looking back now, what did those early romantic experiences teach you about love?

• Your beliefs then

• How views changed

First Meeting

That moment is forever clear – when your grandmother first caught my eye. Something about her told me this meeting would change my life forever.

How did you and Grandma's paths first cross? Share about that initial encounter – the circumstances, your first impressions, and the spark that started it all.

Where and when did you first notice Grandma?

· Exact location

· Special moment

How did you start your first conversation?

· Opening words

· Common interests

What caught your attention about Grandma?

· First attraction

· Strong impression

Early Dates

Dating was different then. Simple pleasures like sharing an ice cream cone or walking in the park held magic.

What were your courtship days like? Remember those special outings, getting to know each other, and the excitement of new love.

Where did you take Grandma on your first date?

• Meeting place

• Time spent

What fun things did you two enjoy doing together?

• Shared hobbies

• Regular outings

What was a memorable date that stands out?

• Special moment

• Lasting memory

Love Letters

Words on paper carried our hearts when we were apart. Those letters, carefully kept, still hold the freshness of young love.

Did you exchange written words of love? Tell about the ways you communicated your feelings and kept in touch.

What special things did you write to each other?

• Written thoughts

• Important words

How often could you communicate back then?

• Contact frequency

• Meeting schedule

Did you keep any special notes or letters?

• Saved messages

• Special cards

Special Places

Certain spots became our own - the diner where we shared sodas, the park bench where we talked for hours, the cinema where we held hands in the dark.

Where did you spend time together while dating? Describe the meaningful locations, favorite spots, and places that hold sweet memories.

Where was your regular meeting spot?

• Meeting point

• Favorite corner

What local spots were popular for couples?

• Dating places

• Youth hangouts

What places became special to you both?

• Important locations

• Meaningful places

Proposal Story

"True love stories never have endings." – Richard Bach

How did you ask Grandma to marry you? Share the details of planning and carrying out your proposal, and her response.

What preparations did you make beforehand?

- Plan details

- Special arrangements

Where and when did you pop the question?

- Exact location

- Time chosen

What was her immediate reaction?

- First response

- Quick answer

Wedding Day

"Marriage is not about finding a person you can live with, it's finding the person you can't live without." - Unknown

How did your wedding day unfold? Tell about the ceremony, celebrations, and special moments that marked the start of your marriage.

What were the key details of your wedding?

- Time chosen

- Main location

What parts of the day stand out most?

- Strong memories

- Special moments

How did you celebrate afterwards?

- Guest activities

- Evening events

First Home

Our first home was modest but it was ours - where we learned to blend two lives into one, where we started building our dreams together.

What was setting up your first home together like? Share about creating your shared space and beginning your life as a couple.

Where was your first place together?

- Home location

- House type

How did you set up your first home?

- Furniture needs

- Space planning

What challenges came with first housekeeping?

- Daily tasks

- Living adjustments

Daily Rhythm

"Love is not about grand gestures. It's about small things done with great love." – Mother Teresa

How did you adjust to married life? Remember establishing routines, sharing responsibilities, and growing together as newlyweds.

How did you spend weekends together?

• Weekend plans

• Regular activities

What traditions did you start early on?

• Special routines

• Family ways

How did you work through disagreements?

• Problem solving

• Talk methods

6

Being a Father

First cries and sleepless nights, tiny hands reaching up to yours. Nothing in life had prepared you for the profound journey of becoming someone's Dad.

Each Child's Birth

"A new baby is like the beginning of all things - wonder, hope, a dream of possibilities." - Eda J. Le Shan

What made each child's arrival unique? Share about the special circumstances and feelings surrounding each of your children's births.

Tell us the story behind each of your children's names. What was special about their names?

• Naming choices

• Name meanings

What was different about welcoming each child?

• Birth moments

• Special conditions

What surprised you most about being a new father?

• Daily challenges

• Learning moments

Unique Talents

Each child brought their own gifts to our family. Watching these talents emerge and grow was life's greatest show.

How did you notice each child's special gifts? Tell about discovering and nurturing their individual abilities and interests.

When did you first notice each child's special interests?

- Early signs

- Natural skills

How did each child show their unique personality?

- Character traits

- Individual styles

What activities brought out their best abilities?

- Special hobbies

- Favorite sports

Teaching Times

Teaching my children wasn't just about lessons - it was showing by example, answering endless questions, helping them discover their own answers.

What important lessons did you share? Describe the ways you taught life skills and values to your children.

What basic skills did you teach your children first?

• Daily tasks

• Practical skills

What family rules were most important to you?

• House rules

• Key values

How did you handle mistakes and misbehavior?

• Teaching methods

• Correction ways

Family Trips

Vacations weren't just destinations. Packed cars, road games, unexpected detours, and shared discoveries created bonds stronger than any souvenir could represent.

Where did you travel as a family? Share about vacation memories and adventures that broadened their horizons.

What was your first big family trip together?

• Travel plans

• Special moments

What unexpected things happened during travels?

• Surprise events

• Funny moments

Which places became family favorites?

• Special spots

• Loved locations

Fun Together

Making time for play mattered as much as any serious lesson – board games, backyard sports, silly moments. These times of pure joy strengthened our family bonds.

What activities brought joy to family time? Remember the games, sports, and entertainment you shared with your children.

What games did your family enjoy playing together?

• Indoor fun

• Outdoor sports

What hobbies did you share with your children?

• Shared interests

• Learning projects

What kind of entertainment did your family enjoy?

• Movie nights

• Music choices

Sports Parent

"Champions aren't made in gyms. Champions are made from something they have deep inside them - a desire, a dream, a vision." - Muhammad Ali

How did you support their athletic interests? Tell about attending games, coaching teams, and encouraging their sports activities.

What sports did each child choose to play?

• Sport choices

• Activity interests

How did you help them practice and improve?

• Training help

• Skill building

How did you handle wins and losses?

• Victory moments

• Tough losses

Proud Moments

Which achievements touched your heart most? Share about times when your children's accomplishments filled you with pride.

What school achievements made you proud?

- Study success

- Academic growth

Which personal goals did they reach?

- Major steps

- Personal wins

What unique talents did they develop?

- Special skills

- Natural gifts

7

Master of the House

Building a home means more than raising walls. You created a sanctuary of love and laughter, where every dinner table conversation wove our family closer together.

House Selection

How did you choose your family home? Share about the search, the decision factors, and the feeling when you knew you'd found the right place.

What was your first family house like, and why did you choose it?

• House features

• Purchase story

What daily routines kept your household running smoothly?

• Morning schedule

• Meal times

What were the favorite gathering spots in your home?

• Family area

• Meal space

Home Improvements

Each project made our house more ours - new paint colors, added rooms, updated features. These improvements weren't just about value, but about crafting spaces for our family's needs.

What changes did you make to your house? Remember the renovations and projects that transformed your house into a home.

Which home changes are you most proud of?

• Major upgrades

• Smart fixes

How did you learn to handle home repairs?

• Fix-it skills

• Tool collection

Which improvements made daily life easier?

• Storage solutions

• Space changes

Garden Growing

Our yard became more than grass and flowers - it was a playground, a gathering space, a source of pride. Each tree and flower bed held stories of family effort and growth.

How did you develop your yard and garden? Tell about landscaping efforts, growing things, and creating outdoor spaces for family enjoyment.

Which plants grew best in your garden?

• Easy growers

• Garden stars

How did you create outdoor spaces for family time?

• Play areas

• Gathering places

What gardening tricks did you learn over time?

• Growing tips

• Pest control

Neighbor Friends

Good neighbors made our street a community - borrowed cups of sugar, shared tools, watched houses, children playing together.

How did you build community connections? Remember the relationships with neighbors and the support network around your home.

What neighborhood activities brought people together?

• Group events

• Shared projects

How did neighbors help each other out?

• Tool sharing

• Emergency aid

What made your neighborhood special?

• Local spots

• Community feel

Seasonal Tasks

Each season brought its own home care rhythm - spring cleaning, summer maintenance, fall preparations, winter weatherizing. These cycles kept our home strong and safe.

What regular maintenance did you manage? Describe the year-round responsibilities of keeping a home running smoothly.

What spring tasks kept your home in shape?

• Garden prep

• Paint jobs

How did you prepare your home for summer?

• AC checks

• Screen repairs

What fall jobs were most important?

• Leaf cleanup

• Gutter work

How did you handle winter home care?

• Snow removal

• Pipe protection

Family Rules

House rules created structure and safety – not just restrictions, but guidelines for respect, responsibility, and living well together.

How did you establish household order? Remember the guidelines and expectations that helped your home run effectively.

What were the basic daily rules in your home?

• Meal times

• Chore duties

What chore system worked best?

• Task lists

• Job rotation

What consequences worked for rule-breaking?

• Fair results

• Clear limits

Quiet Evenings

After daily bustle came peaceful times – reading corners, soft conversations, shared silence. These calm moments balanced our active family life.

What made evening time special? Tell about winding down the day and creating peaceful moments at home.

What was your typical evening schedule?

• Dinner timing

• Night routine

How did family members share evening time?

• Talk moments

• TV shows

Which evening memories stand out most?

• Special nights

• Shared moments

8

Growing Family Tree

Watching your children become parents themselves opened a new chapter. Now your loving influence spans generations, creating ripples through time that keep expanding.

Each grandchild

Every new grandchild brought fresh wonder – each adding new colors to our family rainbow. The heart keeps expanding to embrace them all.

How has each grandchild enriched your life? Remember the unique circumstances and joy surrounding each new grandchild's arrival.

How did you prepare your home for grandchildren visits?

• Safety changes

• Play spaces

Which holidays became more special with grandchildren?

• Family gatherings

• Holiday fun

How do you keep in touch when grandchildren are away?

• Phone chats

• Video calls

Story Times

Every story shared builds bridges. These stories weave them into our larger family tapestry.

What stories do you tell your grandchildren? Tell about sharing family history, personal experiences, and life wisdom through storytelling.

What childhood stories do your grandchildren ask for most?

- Family tales

- Fun adventures

How do you share stories about their parents growing up?

- Kid moments

- Funny mistakes

Which family history stories interest them most?

- Old relatives

- Special events

Teaching Skills

Teaching grandchildren brings different joy - whether fishing, gardening, or simple tasks. There's pleasure in passing skills across generations.

What abilities do you pass down? Remember teaching your grandchildren practical skills and watching them learn and grow.

What everyday skills do you enjoy teaching grandchildren?

• Tool use

• Fix things

How do you share your hobby skills with them?

• Project time

• Hands-on work

What problem-solving skills do you demonstrate?

• Think ahead

• Smart choices

Holiday Magic

Holidays shine brighter with grandchildren - their wonder refreshes familiar celebrations, their joy makes traditions new again.

How do you make family gatherings special? Share about creating memorable celebrations and traditions with the extended family.

What makes holiday gatherings at your house unique?

• Special setup

• Family spots

What holiday traditions started with grandchildren?

• Gift customs

• Special games

What seasonal activities do you plan?

• Summer fun

• Winter games

Individual Time

One-on-one moments with each grandchild are precious - building unique bonds, understanding their special qualities, creating memories just for us.

What activities do you enjoy with each grandchild? Tell about building unique bonds and connecting one-on-one with each grandchild.

What unique interests do you share with each grandchild?

• Special games

• Shared likes

What special places do you visit together?

• Local spots

• Secret places

How do you make each grandchild feel special?

• Private talks

• Own space

Modern Ways

Their world differs from my youth, yet basic truths remain - about love, character, and family. Bridging these differences enriches us both.

How do you bridge traditional and modern? Describe adapting to current times while sharing timeless values with your grandchildren.

How has technology changed how you connect?

- Video calls

- Text chats

What new things have grandchildren taught you?

- Tech help

- New games

How do you blend old and new activities?

- Mixed hobbies

- Fresh ways

Love Language

Love speaks differently with grandchildren - through patience, presence, gentle guidance, unconditional acceptance. It's love without burden or expectation.

How do you express grandfather love? Describe the special ways you show affection and care for your grandchildren.

What special greetings do you share?

• Hello ways

• Welcome signs

What comfort routines have you created?

• Quiet times

• Cozy spots

How do you show support at their events?

• Show up

• Watch games

9

A Man's Pursuits

Beyond work and family duties, these were the passions that made your eyes light up. Every hobby and interest revealed another fascinating layer of who you are.

Weekend Passions

Weekends were for pursuing what brought joy – those activities that refreshed the spirit and balanced work life.

What activities filled your free time? Share about the hobbies and interests that made weekends special and refreshing.

What hobbies have stayed with you through different stages of life?

• Long-term interests

• Favorite pastimes

Which hobby tools or equipment do you treasure most?

• Special gear

• Collection pieces

What new hobbies have you picked up recently?

• Fresh starts

• Late discoveries

Tool Collection

Each tool in my workshop tells a story. They're more than imple-ments; they're partners in creation, each with its own history.

What's the story of your workshop tools? Tell about gathering your equipment, learning to use each tool, and the projects they helped create.

What's the most useful tool you've ever bought?

- Best investment

- Daily helper

How did you build your workshop over time?

- Smart choices

- Space planning

Which tools have interesting repair stories?

- Fix attempts

- Tool saves

Building Projects

Each project built more than objects - it built confidence, problem-solving skills, and satisfaction in creation. The process mattered as much as results.

What did you construct or create? Tell about significant DIY projects and the pride of building things with your own hands.

What was your first major building project?

• First challenge

• Starting skills

Which project gave you the most trouble?

• Tough spots

• Smart fixes

What project would you still like to build?

• Dream builds

• Bucket list

Sports Following

Following sports wasn't just about scores – it was about loyalty, tradition, sharing victories and defeats. These teams became part of our family's rhythm and conversation.

Which teams and sports captured your interest? Remember the games, players, and memorable moments you've followed over the years.

How did you choose your favorite teams?

• Home teams

• Family influence

Which players did you most admire?

• Star athletes

• Sports heroes

What's your most exciting sports memory?

• Victory moment

• Amazing plays

Nature Time

How did outdoor activities enrich your life? Describe your experiences in nature, from hiking to gardening to wildlife watching.

What's your favorite outdoor activity through the seasons?

• Yearly plans

• Season spots

What's your most memorable wildlife encounter?

• Animal meetings

• Nature spots

What outdoor skills proved most valuable?

• Tool use

• Safety knowledge

Movie Nights

"Movies touch our hearts and awaken our vision, and change the way we see things." - Martin Scorsese

What films have meant the most? Remember favorite movies and the stories that entertained or inspired you over time.

What was your first memorable movie experience?

• First theater

• Special film

Which film heroes inspired you?

• Screen characters

• Story impacts

What movies do you enjoy sharing?

• Family picks

• Share moments

Reading Choice

"Reading is to the mind what exercise is to the body." - Joseph Ad-dison

What kinds of books drew you in? Share about your favorite authors, subjects, and how reading has influenced your life.

Which book would you read again right now?

- Top picks

- Time favorites

Which authors became your trusted favorites?

- Regular reads

- Book series

How has your reading taste changed?

- Interest shifts

- Genre changes

Music Moments

Certain songs marked life's chapters - dancing with your grand-mother, children's lullabies, family singalongs. Music wove through our happiest times.

What songs and performances moved you? Tell about the music that's been meaningful and how it's enhanced your life experiences.

What was your first favorite song or artist?

• Early tunes

• Music discovery

Which concerts stand out in your memory?

• Live shows

• Performance magic

How did you listen to music over time?

• Music players

• Sound systems

Club Friends

Sharing interests with others enriched the experience – whether bowling leagues, veteran groups, or community clubs. These connections added depth to hobbies.

What groups or clubs were you part of? Share about the social connections and shared interests that brought people together.

Which club activities were most enjoyable?

• Group events

• Fun times

What did you learn from club experiences?

• Skill gains

• People lessons

How have your social groups changed?

• Time shifts

• New circles

Collection Pride

Starting collections wasn't about gathering things - it was about preserving history, appreciating craftsmanship, connecting to past times.

What items did you enjoy collecting? Tell about gathering and preserving special items that held meaning for you.

How did you start your first collection?

• First piece

• Start moment

What makes certain pieces extra special?

• Rare finds

• Story items

How do you organize your collections?

• Display methods

• Storage tricks

Travel Adventures

"Travel makes one modest. You see what a tiny place you occupy in the world." – Gustav Flaubert

Where did your journeys take you? Share about memorable trips, discoveries, and places that left lasting impressions.

Which place surprised you most?

- Unexpected finds

- Culture shock

Which local foods stand out?

- Taste memories

- Food finds

What place keeps calling you back?

- Return spots

- Magic places

10

From My Heart to Yours

Your journey has carved wisdom into your heart. Now, share your hopes, dreams and life lessons – gifts more precious than gold for generations to come.

Greatest Lessons

Life's most important teachings came not from books but from living
– through triumph and failure, joy and sorrow. These lessons became
the compass points of my journey.

What fundamental truths have shaped your life? Share the most important insights you've gained through your years of experience.

What's the best advice you ever received and still follow today?

• Trusted guidance

• Lasting impact

Which mistake taught you the most valuable lesson?

• Learning moment

• Better path

What habit or practice has served you well through life?

• Daily routine

• Steady progress

Peace Found

Inner peace came through acceptance – of self, of others, of life's flow.
This peace became strength during storms and joy during calm.

What brings true contentment? Remember discovering sources of inner peace and maintaining strength through life's challenges.

What daily activity helps you feel most peaceful?

• Peaceful activity

• Quiet moment

Where do you go when you need to clear your mind?

• Special place

• Quiet corner

What hobby helps you forget your worries?

• Relaxing activity

• Joy work

Faith Matter

Let faith anchor your life - in something greater than yourself, in goodness prevailing, in love's power to transform.

What spiritual guidance would you share? Tell them about finding and following their beliefs and values.

When did faith become important in your life?

• First belief

• Important moment

What daily practice strengthens your faith?

• Daily faith

• Spirit care

How does faith help during tough times?

• Tough time help

• Hard day comfort

Balanced Life

"Life is not measured by the number of breaths we take, but by the moments that take our breath away." - Maya Angelou

What creates a well-balanced life? Tell about finding harmony between work, family, personal time, and other life aspects.

How do you divide time between work and family?

- Family time

- Work balance

How do you recharge when feeling tired?

- Energy boost

- Quick recovery

What activity helps you stay healthy?

- Body care

- Strong habits

Dream Big

Never let anyone dim your dreams - they're the seeds of tomorrow's reality. Believe in possibilities, trust your heart's whispers, reach beyond what seems possible.

What encouragement would you offer? Share your hopes for their dreams and advice about reaching for their goals.

What childhood dream actually came true?

• Early goal

• Dream success

What helped you stay confident?

• Keep going

• Self trust

What dream still drives you today?

• Current goal

• Future hope

Future Hope

Your future holds possibilities I can't imagine – embrace change, stay curious, keep learning. The world needs your unique gifts.

What dreams do you hold for them? Share your wishes and hopes for their future happiness and success.

What adventure do you wish your grandchildren to experience?

- Adventure hope

- Travel dream

What strength do you see growing in them?

- Special talent

- Growing strength

What happiness do you dream for their future?

- Happy life

- Heart peace

Grandma's Edition Available

Grandma, I Want to Hear About Your Life

Ever wonder about the young girl who became your cherished grandmother? The magic of her first love story? The wisdom gathered through decades of nurturing generations? This heart-warming companion to our Grandpa edition opens another precious window into your family's legacy.

Through thoughtfully crafted chapters, discover the gentle strength and timeless grace of your grandmother's journey. Every page captures the essence of a life filled with love and tender moments.

Our "Family Story" collection also includes the beloved **Mom and Dad editions**.

Don't let these treasured tales slip away. Give a gift that will warm hearts for generations to come. Because every grandmother's story is a legacy of love worth preserving.

Available at major online bookstores:

- Amazon

- Barnes & Noble

- and other leading online retailers

www.ingramcontent.com/pod-product-compliance
Lightning Source LLC
Chambersburg PA
CBHW051324120626
46547CB00015B/2380